User's Guide
to
The Bluebook

Revised for the nineteenth edition

Alan L. Dworsky

References updated by Brian Christiansen

William S. Hein & Co., Inc.
Buffalo, New York
2010

Library of Congress Cataloging-in-Publication Data
Dworsky, Alan L.
    User's guide to the Bluebook / Alan L. Dworsky ; references
updated by Brian Christiansen — Rev. for the 19th ed.
        p. cm.
    Includes bibliographical references.
    ISBN 978-0-8377-3838-3 (paper : alk. paper)
        1. Citation of legal authorities—United States. I. Christiansen,
Brian. II. Bluebook. 19th ed. III. Title.
    KF245.D853 2010
    348.73'47—dc22   2010030059

To Betsy and Molly

For copies of this book or other books by
Alan L. Dworsky, please contact the publisher:

William S. Hein & Co., Inc.
1285 Main Street / Buffalo, NY 14209
(800) 828-7571 / www.wshein.com

Printed in the United States of America

This volume is printed on acid-free paper.

Contents

1 Introduction

Correct citation form, like correct spelling, is a superficial but important sign to a reader about your trustworthiness as a writer. And despite some serious competition in recent years, the *Bluebook* is still the dominant authority on citation form.

But the nineteenth edition—like its predecessors—is too long, too complicated, and too picky. Its main problem is that it's really two books in one. It has one set of typeface rules for writers of law review articles and treatises and another set of rules for practitioners—law students, law clerks, lawyers, legal secretaries, and paralegals—writing memoranda and briefs.

This *User's Guide* is written for practitioners, and it should make your task of mastering citation form as easy and painless as possible. To help you use this guide along with the *Bluebook*, I've listed the numbers of the relevant *Bluebook* rules under most chapter subheadings. But you may find that once you learn the rules in this guide, you'll only need the *Bluebook* for its tables and for that one weird citation you do each year.

2   A Quick Tour of the *Bluebook*

The *Bluebook* puts on weight with every new edition. It's now an intimidating 511 pages long. You ask: How am I ever going to learn 511 pages of citation rules? You're not. The actual rules of citation form are contained on less than half the *Bluebook*'s pages. And the rules for practitioners are summarized in the section called the Bluepages, which has only 25 pages of rules.

A good way to get an idea of the organization of the *Bluebook* is to keep the book closed and hold it up so you can see the right side, the side where you can flip through the pages. You'll see four main sections identified by the color of the edges of the pages.

The first section is light blue. That's the section of rules for practitioners like you—the Bluepages. The second section is white; that's the main section of rules. The third and largest section looks dark blue, but the color comes only from a stripe at the edges of the pages. That's the section of tables, and the pages in it are actually white. The fourth and smallest section is white like the section of rules; that's the index, and it's excellent.

Now open the book to the Bluepages, which start on page 3. The rules in the Bluepages are abbreviated B1, B2, B3, etc. You'll find rule numbers in the margin at the start of each rule and at the top of each page in the outside corner.

The Bluepages tables start on page 28. Bluepages table 1 (BT1) contains abbreviations of words used in the titles of court documents. Bluepages table 2 (BT2) contains a list of citation rules from specific jurisdictions, and whenever those local rules differ from *Bluebook* rules, the local rules take precedence.

The main section of rules in the *Bluebook* starts on page 53. These rules are abbreviated R1, R2, R3, etc. Again, you'll find rule numbers in the margin at the start of each rule and at the top of each page in the outside corner.

The section of tables begins on page 215. These tables are abbreviated T1, T2, T3, etc. The most important table is the first one—table T1—which covers the United States. It's divided into four sections. Federal courts and laws are covered in Tables T1.1 and T1.2 on pages 215–28. The states, arranged alphabetically, are covered in Table T1.3 on pages 228–74.

The tables of abbreviations start with table T6 on page 430. If you're scanning for a particular table of abbreviations, you'll find the names at the top of each page along with the table numbers.

On the last page of the *Bluebook* and on the inside of the back cover, you'll find samples of citations in the form you need for legal memoranda and briefs This guide is basically an explanation and expansion of what you see on those two pages.

3 Typeface

Citations in memoranda and briefs use only two kinds of typeface: ordinary typeface and underlined typeface. Large and small caps are used in law review footnotes, but not in memoranda and briefs. In fact, you shouldn't be using footnotes for your citations at all; your citations should appear in the body of your text.

The *Bluebook* says practitioners can use italics instead of underlining. But most practitioners have traditionally used underlining, and all the *Bluebook* examples for practitioners use underlining exclusively. Because your computer will produce ordinary typeface automatically, all you have to learn is what to underline.

What to Underline
Bluepages B1

Here are the things that must be underlined:

1. case names (including any procedural phrase at the beginning of a case name, such as "<u>ex parte</u>" or "<u>in re</u>");
2. titles of books and articles;
3. titles of legislative materials (other than bills) that have them;
4. titles of publications not normally underlined (such as reporters or law reviews) when you refer to them in textual sentences without citing them;
5. introductory signals (such as "<u>see, e.g.,</u>" or "<u>accord</u>") used in citation sentences or clauses;
6. explanatory phrases introducing prior or subsequent history (such as "<u>aff'd</u>," "<u>rev'd</u>," or "<u>cert. denied</u>");
7. words and phrases introducing related authority (such as "<u>in</u>," "<u>quoted in</u>," or "<u>citing</u>");

4

8. cross-references ("<u>Id.</u>," "<u>supra</u>," and "<u>infra</u>," but not "hereinafter");
9. foreign words not commonly found in legal writing;
10. words italicized in the original of a quotation.

In addition, you can underline anything you want to emphasize in your writing.

Whenever something on this list consists of two or more words, make your underline continuous. Only break the underline between two different things that are next to each other, such as an introductory signal and a case name:

Example 1

<u>See, e.g.</u>, <u>Schoenfield v. First Commodity Corp.</u>, 793 F.2d 28 (1st Cir. 1986).

Because "<u>See, e.g.</u>" constitutes one introductory signal, the underline under it is continuous. The underline under the case name is also continuous. But between the introductory signal and the case name there is a break in the underlining.

What Not to Underline
Bluepages B1

Everything else. This includes:

1. constitutions;
2. statutes;
3. restatements;
4. names of reporters and services;
5. model codes;
6. rules;
7. executive orders;
8. administrative materials.

These eight categories, and anything else you can think of, are printed in ordinary typeface in memoranda and briefs.

4 How to Cite a Case
Rule 10

State Cases

Regional reporters
Rule 10.3; Bluepages B4.1

Even though more and more legal research is being done online, citation rules still require that you cite to a traditional hard copy source. For state court cases, often the only source you have to cite is a regional reporter. A reporter is a collection of cases bound together in a book. The regional reporters are multi-volume sets published by West. They include the *Atlantic, Pacific, North Eastern, South Eastern, Southern, North Western,* and *South Western Reporters.* Each contains cases from several states.

In a basic citation to a case found in a reporter, you're trying to convey four pieces of information efficiently:

1. the name of the case;
2. where the case can be found;
3. the court that decided the case;
4. the year the case was decided.

The name of the case comes first, followed by where it can be found. The court and the year come last in parentheses.

For example, take the following citation:

Example 2
<u>Clemens v. Wilcox</u>, 392 N.W.2d 863 (Minn. 1986).

"<u>Clemens v. Wilcox</u>" is the name of the case. It should always be underlined. "392 N.W.2d 863" tells where the case can be found: in volume 392 of the *North Western Reporter* second series at page 863. Notice that there are no spaces in "N.W.2d."

The "Minn." in the parentheses tells you that the case was decided by the Minnesota Supreme Court. How do you know that? Because an abbreviation of the name of the state in the parentheses *with no other abbreviation added* indicates that the case was decided by the highest court in the state.

A full list of abbreviations of state names can be found in the *Bluebook* in table T10. You'll also find these abbreviations in parentheses after the name of each state's highest court in table T1. Only Alaska, Idaho, Iowa, Ohio, and Utah are written out in full.

If the case was decided by a court other than the highest court in the state, then the abbreviation of the name of the court must be added to the abbreviation of the name of the state. For example, the New Mexico Court of Appeals is "N.M. Ct. App.," the Connecticut Appellate Court is "Conn. App. Ct.," and the Delaware Court of Chancery is "Del. Ch." The abbreviations of the names of lower state courts can be found in parentheses after the names of the courts in table T1.

Finally, the "1986" in the parentheses in the citation tells you the court decided the case in 1986. Sometimes the heading at the beginning of a case gives other dates, such as the date the case was filed or the date review or rehearing was denied. If all the dates aren't in the same year, use the year given at the top of the pages of the case.

Memorize the punctuation for a basic case citation. The name of the case is followed by a comma, but there is no comma between the page number on which the case appears ("863" in Example 2 on page 6) and the parentheses containing the name of the court and the year. There also is no comma within the parentheses between the name of the court and the year. Finally, note that "versus" is abbreviated as "v." in case names, not "vs."

If a state case doesn't appear in a regional reporter, the section on the state in table T1 will give you alternative reporters to cite and their abbreviations. The name of each reporter is given on the left side of the page, the dates covered by the reporter are given in the middle, and the abbreviation of the name of the reporter is given on the right.

If you want to cite a court that doesn't appear in table T1, abbreviate its name using table T7 as a guide.

Official state reporters
Rule 10.3; Bluepages table BT2

When you submit a memorandum or brief to a state court, you must follow any local rules on citation form. Usually a state's local rules concern how to cite decisions of that state's courts. They typically require that a case be cited to the official state reporter—the reporter published by the state itself or by a statutorily authorized publisher. Sometimes they require a parallel citation to an unofficial reporter such as the West regional reporters. You'll find a list of these "jurisdiction-specific citation rules" in Bluepages table BT2.

For example, Arizona appellate rules require that Arizona cases be cited to the official state reporter and to an unofficial reporter if possible. So a citation to a case decided by the Arizona Supreme Court submitted in a memorandum or brief to that court would look like this:

Example 3
Carroll v. Lee, 148 Ariz. 10, 712 P.2d 923 (1986).

When you give parallel citations for a state case, the citation to the official state reporter comes first. The official state reporter for Arizona Supreme Court cases is the Arizona Reports, which is abbreviated "Ariz." according to the section on Arizona in table T1 of the *Bluebook*. The names of almost all official state reporters consist of the name of the state followed by "Reports."

The exceptions are mainly old reporters—usually originating in the 19th century—that were named for whoever compiled them.

When the abbreviated name of the official reporter is the same as the abbreviated name of the highest court in the state, you don't need to put anything in the parentheses with the year. The name of the reporter takes the place of the name of the court. That's why there's nothing in the parentheses with "1986" in Example 3 above. Even when a reporter has more than one series and therefore has an ordinal in its abbreviated name (such as "Cal. 3d" or "Wis. 2d"), its name is still treated as being the same as the name of the highest court in the state.

When you give parallel citations for a case decided by a state court other than the highest court in a state, you should omit the abbreviated name of the state from the parentheses if the information is conveyed by the name of the official reporter:

Example 4

Tobias v. Dailey, 196 Ariz. 418, 998 P.2d 1091 (Ct. App. 2000).

By combining "Ariz." from "196 Ariz. 418" with "Ct. App." from within the parentheses, the reader can tell the case was decided by the Arizona Court of Appeals. And if the name of the official reporter also conveys the name of the court, you can also omit the abbreviated name of the court from the parentheses:

Example 5

Lang v. Jones, 36 Colo. App. 29, 535 P.2d 242 (1975).

Federal Cases

Rule 10.4(a); Bluepages B4.1

The rules that follow cover most federal court cases you'll cite as a law student or as a lawyer in general practice. For specialized federal courts (including the United States Claims Court, the Bank-

ruptcy Courts, and the Tax Court) and for very old federal cases,
see rule 10.4(a) and the tables for the federal courts in table T1.

The United States Supreme Court

The *Bluebook* tells you in table T1.1 to cite only the official
reporter for United States Supreme Court opinions. That reporter
is the *United States Reports,* abbreviated "U.S.":

Example 6
Pulley v. Harris, 465 U.S. 37 (1984).

Since the *United States Reports* contains only opinions of the
Supreme Court, you don't have to identify the Supreme Court
anywhere in the citation. That's why in Example 8 only the year
appears in the parentheses.

If a Supreme Court opinion doesn't appear in the *United States
Reports,* then cite the *Supreme Court Reporter* (S. Ct.). If it
doesn't appear there either, cite the *United States Supreme Court
Reports—Lawyer's Edition* (L. Ed. or L. Ed. 2d). If it doesn't
appear in any of these three reporters, cite the periodical *United
States Law Week* (U.S.L.W.).

The rule that you can't give a parallel citation to a Supreme
Court case is commonly ignored. Most lawyers and courts
(including the Supreme Court itself) add parallel citations to both
S. Ct. and L. Ed. 2d.

The federal courts of appeals

The federal courts of appeals have no official reporter, so they are
cited to West's *Federal Reporter* (F., F.2d, or F.3d). Give the
name of the court in the parentheses with the year, and abbreviate
that name as "Cir." with an ordinal: 1st Cir., 2d Cir., 3d Cir., 4th
Cir., etc.:

Example 7
Valdez v. Black, 446 F.2d 1071 (10th Cir. 1971).

Note that there's no space between "F." and "2d" in "F.2d." Under rule 6.1(a) on spacing, you generally aren't supposed to put a space between single capital letters, and an ordinal such as "2d" is treated as a single capital letter. Also note that the *Bluebook* spells the ordinals for "second" and "third" as "2d" and "3d," not "2nd" and "3rd."

Remember that the abbreviations of court names given in the *Bluebook* are only for citations. Don't use abbreviated words or ordinals in a textual sentence:

Example 8
This issue has been decided recently by the Tenth Circuit.

The federal district courts

The federal district courts also have no official reporter. Since 1932, federal district court opinions have appeared in West's *Federal Supplement* (F. Supp. or F. Supp. 2d). Identify the court and abbreviate its name in the parentheses with the year:

Example 9
Michaels v. New Jersey, 50 F. Supp. 2d 353 (D.N.J. 1999).

In Example 9, "D.N.J." stands for "District of New Jersey." This is the abbreviation for the name of the federal district court for the district of New Jersey. All federal district courts are abbreviated with a "D." followed by the name of the state in which the court is located.

New Jersey has only one district, but some states have more than one. For those states, add a letter indicating the district (such as "S." for "Southern") before the "D." for "District" in the abbreviated name of the court. For example, the Federal District Court for the Eastern District of Virginia would be abbreviated "E.D. Va."

Although you must identify the particular district of a federal district court, you shouldn't add the name of a particular division within a district.

Other Sources for Cases

LEXIS, Westlaw, and the Internet
Rules 10.3.1(b) and 18.3.1

If a case isn't available as an official public domain citation or in a published reporter, the next best place to cite it is to a widely used electronic database like LEXIS or Westlaw. Here are the elements of a citation to an electronic database in the order they should be given:

1. the case name;
2. the number of the case assigned by the court;
3. the year the case was decided;
4. the database identifier (like LEXIS or WL for Westlaw);
5. the number or identifying code assigned to the case by the database (if there is one);
6. the abbreviated name of the court (in parentheses);
7. the full date (in the parentheses with the abbreviated name of the court—see table T12 for the abbreviations to use for the name of a month in a full date).

Here's a citation to a case on LEXIS:

Example 10

Coteau Servs. v. Alexis, Inc., No. 86-5296, 1988 U.S. Dist. LEXIS 1019 (E.D. La. Feb. 10, 1988).

And here's a citation to the same case on Westlaw:

Example 11

<u>Coteau Servs. v. Alexis, Inc.</u>, No. 86-5296, 1988 WL 10171 (E.D. La. Feb. 10, 1988).

If an authority isn't available in a printed source or an electronic database like LEXIS or Westlaw, as a last resort you can cite the Internet. You can also use the Internet as a parallel citation if it will substantially improve access to the authority. When you do that, use the explanatory phrase "<u>available at</u>" before the web site address:

Example 12

Pistoria v. Pistoria, No. C4-00-304, 2000 WL 1219435 (Minn. Ct. App. Aug. 29, 2000), <u>available at</u> http://www.courts.stat.mn. us/opinions/coa/current/coacur.html.

Looseleaf services
Rules 10.3.1(b) and 19

After electronic databases, the next best source to cite is a looseleaf service. Looseleaf services are so named because they usually consist of ringed binders that are updated frequently with inserts. They often contain cases and administrative materials in a single area of law.

When you cite a case to a looseleaf service, give the following in this order:

1. the name of the case;
2. the volume number or name;
3. the name of the service and publisher abbreviated according to table T15, with the abbreviated name of the publisher in parentheses;
4. the paragraph or other subdivision number;
5. the abbreviated name of the court (in parentheses);
6. the exact date the case was decided (in the parentheses with the name of the court).

Thus:

Example 13
```
Hayes v. Sampson, [1980 Transfer Binder]
Fed. Sec. L. Rep. (CCH) ¶ 97,693 (S.D.N.Y.
Nov. 18, 1980).
```

"Fed. Sec. L. Rep. (CCH)" in Example 13 is the abbreviation for the *Federal Securities Law Reports* published by Commerce Clearing House. Brackets are around "1980 Transfer Binder" because rule 3.1(a) says to put the volume designation in brackets whenever it includes words. Rule 19 contains other rules for citing services.

Public domain citations
Rule 10.3.3

An official public domain citation is a citation to a case published by a court rather than a private company like West. If a state court case has a public domain citation, rule 10.3.1(b) requires that you use it. This rule will pose practical problems for the foreseeable future because public domain citations are only widely available online from state court web sites and services like Westlaw and LEXIS. If your primary research will be conducted in printed sources like regional reporters, you may want to check whether your assignment includes the extra work of tracking down public domain citations online.

The format of public domain citations varies from jurisdiction to jurisdiction, so you need to check the section on the state in table T1 to make sure you get it right. For example, here's a public domain citation to a case decided by the South Dakota Supreme Court. It contains the name of the case, the year the case was decided, the abbreviation for the name of the court, and the number assigned to the case, in that order:

Example 14

<u>Atkins v. Stratmeyer</u>, 1999 SD 131.

Notice that since the case was decided by the highest court in the state, all that's needed in the citation is an abbreviation of the name of the state. But also notice that South Dakota is abbreviated "SD"—without periods—rather than "S.D." State court public domain citations often use the state's two-letter postal code rather than the abbreviations in table T10.1.

If a state case with a public domain citation also appears in a regional reporter, you have to give both citations. Citing an authority to more than one source is called giving "parallel citations." When you give parallel citations for a state case, the public domain citation comes first, followed by the citation to the regional reporter:

Example 15

<u>Atkins v. Stratmeyer</u>, 1999 SD 131, 600 N.W.2d 891.

Notice that there's no parenthetical at the end of the parallel citation to the regional reporter. Since the public domain citation already lets the reader know what court decided the case and in what year, including that information in the parallel citation would be redundant.

Other Rules for Citing Cases

Subsequent and prior history

Rule 10.7; Bluepages B4.1.6

When you cite a case, you'll usually be citing its final disposition. But if something happened in a case after the version you're citing, you must give that subsequent history when you cite the case in full, subject to some exceptions in rule 10.7. Introduce the subsequent history with an abbreviated explanatory phrase and underline the abbreviation:

Example 16

Community Nutrition Inst. v. Block, 698
F.2d 1239 (D.C. Cir. 1983), rev'd, 467 U.S.
340 (1984).

In Example 16, "rev'd" is the abbreviation for "reversed." A list of the most commonly used explanatory phrases in their abbreviated forms appears in table T8. Note that there's no period at the end of "rev'd" or the other abbreviations in table T8 that are constructed by omitting letters from *within* a word rather than at the end of a word.

The case in Example 16 had a different name in the Supreme Court; there it was "Block v. Community Nutrition Inst." Because the names of the parties were merely reversed, I didn't indicate this difference. But if the case name had been different in any other way, I would have had to indicate that in the subsequent history by adding "sub nom." (which means "under the name of") after "rev'd" and then by giving the different case name, as in the following example:

Example 17

Tensile Steel Corp. v. Sather, 715 F. Supp.
514 (D. Colo. 1989), rev'd sub nom. Tensile
Res. v. Sather, 913 F.2d 846 (10th Cir.
1990).

You don't have to give the prior history of a case unless it's important to the point you're making with the case. If you give both the prior and subsequent history of a case, give the prior before the subsequent.

You must look closely at the explanatory phrases "rev'd" and "rev'g" because they appear so similar. The same is true for "aff'd" and "aff'g." For example, "*A*, aff'd *B*" gives a subsequent history; the *A* case was affirmed by the *B* case. "*A*, aff'g *B*" gives a prior history; the *A* case affirmed the *B* case.

Introductory signals
Rule 1.2; Bluepages B3

Introductory signals explain how you are using a particular case or other authority. A list of introductory signals and their meanings appears on pages 54–56 in the *Bluebook*.

A citation in a memorandum or brief is strongest when it is preceded by no signal at all. That means the cited authority directly states the proposition the citation follows. It can also mean the cited authority is the authority you've just referred to or quoted in your text. If you're using a case in any other way, it's best to explain how in your text. Introductory signals are usually too imprecise to do the job.

If you do use an introductory signal, remember to underline it:

Example 18
```
Accord Frye v. Memphis State Univ., 806
S.W.2d 170 (Tenn. 1991).
```

No comma separates the signal from the rest of the citation, except after "e.g." If you use "e.g." with another signal, you have to put a comma both before and after it, as in Example 1 on page 5.

Parentheticals
Rules 1.5 and 10.6; Bluepages B4.1.5

You can say anything you want in parentheses following a citation (as opposed to an introductory signal, where you're limited to the list in the *Bluebook*). For example, following a case citation, you can briefly explain the proposition the case stands for or summarize the facts of the case:

Example 19
```
Pine River State Bank v. Mettle, 333 N.W.2d
622 (Minn. 1983) (employee handbook can
constitute contract).
```

Example 20

Pine River State Bank v. Mettle, 333 N.W.2d
622 (Minn. 1983) (fired bank employee
claimed discharge breached terms of
employee handbook).

Note that the first word in a parenthetical is not capitalized and
that the final period comes after the last parenthesis.

Don't put the facts of a case that's important to your discussion or argument in a parenthetical. Parentheticals work best for the facts of a series of cases serving as additional support on a point for which you have other, more important authority:

Example 21

Courts in other jurisdictions have held
that a delay of a month or less in making
repairs can cause a limited remedy to fail
of its essential purpose: Albeniz v.
Cullton Tractor, 516 A.2d 823 (N.H. 1986)
(remedy failed where tractor not repaired
for ten days); Shorter v. Allied Indus.,
426 N.W.2d 877 (Iowa 1988) (remedy failed
where drill press not repaired for two
weeks); Systems Design v. AAA Boiler Co.,
737 P.2d 619 (Ore. 1987) (remedy failed
where boiler not repaired for three weeks).

If you rely on a dissenting opinion, you must disclose that in a parenthetical:

Example 22

An owner of a housing development can also
be a contractor for purposes of workers'
compensation. Mayhew v. Howell, 401 S.E.2d
831, 834 (N.C. Ct. App. 1991) (Phillips,
J., dissenting).

Parentheticals come directly after the citation to the case they refer to, before any prior or subsequent history:

Example 23

Community Nutrition Inst. v. Block, 698
F.2d 1239 (D.C. Cir. 1983) (individual
consumers have standing to challenge milk
regulations), rev'd, 467 U.S. 340 (1984).

Rule 10.6 gives other rules on the use of parentheticals in case citations. Rule 1.5 gives other rules on the use of parentheticals in citations to any authority.

Location and order of citations
Rules 1.1 and 1.4; Bluepages B3.5

When a citation applies to the entire preceding sentence or sentences, it can stand alone as a separate sentence (called a "citation sentence"):

Example 24

An employee handbook can constitute a
contract. Pine River State Bank v. Mettle,
333 N.W.2d 622 (Minn. 1983).

Citation sentences like the one in Example 24 are the best place for your citations. They keep your citations out of the way, where they don't break the flow of what you're saying or make your sentences hard to follow.

If you use a citation that applies to only part of a sentence, put it immediately after the part it applies to and set it off with commas:

Example 25

An employee handbook can constitute a
contract, Pine River State Bank v. Mettle,
333 N.W.2d 622 (Minn. 1983), but this rule
should not apply to an employee newsletter.

When a citation appears in the middle of a sentence, as in Example 25, it's called a "citation clause." But the sentence in Example 25 would be better rewritten as two sentences, so the reader wouldn't have to climb over that boulder in the middle of it.

When you cite more than one case or authority, separate the citations with semicolons:

Example 26

```
An employee can constitute a contract. Pine
River State Bank v. Mettle, 333 N.W.2d 622
(Minn. 1983); Kulkay v. Allied Stores, 398
N.W.2d 573 (Minn. Ct. App. 1986).
```

Also, when you cite more than one case or authority, put them in order of their importance to your point, starting with the most important. If you are citing cases of equal importance, rule 1.4(d) gives the order to put them in. Start with the highest court and work down. List cases decided by the same court in reverse chronological order. Federal courts come before state courts.

In Example 26, I put Pine River before Kulkay because Pine River was the more important case. If the two cases were of equal importance to the point I was making, I still would have put Pine River first because it was decided by the higher court.

Rule 1.4 gives similar rules for citing other authority. Constitutions come before statutes. Statutes come before cases. Cases come before what your Uncle Herman says at the dinner table. These and other kinds of authority are further broken down into subcategories in rule 1.4 and listed in the order in which they should be cited. But remember that all these ordering rules apply only when your authorities are of equal importance to your point.

Case names
Rules 10.2 and 10.2.1; Bluepages B4.1.1

The *Bluebook* has two sets of rules for case names: one for case names in textual sentences and one for case names in citations. Luckily, the only difference between the two is that more words must be abbreviated in citations.

In textual sentences, the only abbreviations you should use in a case name are widely known acronyms such as "NAACP" and the following eight abbreviations: "&," "Ass'n," "Bros.," "Co.," "Corp.," "Inc.," Ltd.," and "No." But don't even use one of these eight if it begins a party's name.

In citations, you must abbreviate each word listed in table T6 and the names of geographical units listed in table T10 (unless it's the entire name of a party). You also *may* abbreviate any word longer than eight letters if it saves you substantial space and the abbreviation is clear.

The following rules apply to *all* case names:

1. Give only the name of the first action listed at the beginning of a case when two or more actions have been consolidated.

2. Give only the name of the first party on each side of the "v.," no matter how many parties there are. Don't add words such as "et al."

3. Give only the last name of a person, except for the unusual situations listed in rule 10.2.1(g).

4. Omit "Inc.," "Ltd.," and similar terms when the name also contains words that make it obvious the party is a business entity. In Example 26 on page 20, the full name of the defendant in <u>Kulkay v. Allied Stores</u> was "Allied Stores, Inc." I omitted the "Inc." from my citation because it was obvious Allied Stores was a business.

5. When a state is a party to a case decided by a court of that state, refer to the state simply as "State," "People," or "Commonwealth" (depending on which one appears in the case name). When a state is a party to a case decided elsewhere, use only the name of the state and omit phrases such as "State of."

6. Abbreviate "The United States of America" as "United States," not "U.S."

You can shrink case names even further in short forms, which are explained below.

Abbreviations of case names printed at the top of the pages in a reporter can give you some guidance on how to abbreviate a particularly long name. But they often do not follow *Bluebook* rules, so don't rely on them blindly.

Short form for case names
Rule 10.9; Bluepages B4.2

After giving the full citation of a case, you may want to refer to the case in your text without citing it. You don't have to repeat the full citation or the full name every time you mention the case. Just use the name of the first party. For example, if the case is <u>Fisher v. Duckworth</u>, you can refer to it like this:

Example 27
```
In Fisher, the court established a new
rule.
```

But remember you can't give a short form of a case name until after you've given the full citation. In the following example, "In <u>Tiedeman</u>" *incorrectly* comes before the full citation of the case:

Example 28
```
In Tiedeman, the court interpreted the
Minnesota Good Samaritan Law. Tiedeman v.
Morgan, 435 N.W.2d 86 (Minn. Ct. App.
1989).
```

The short form *correctly* appears for the first time after the full citation in the following example:

Example 29
```
The court has recently interpreted the
Minnesota Good Samaritan Law. Tiedeman v.
Morgan, 435 N.W.2d 86 (Minn. Ct. App.
1989). In Tiedeman, the court held the
```

```
statute supplemented the common-law duty to
rescue.
```

If a government or some other frequent litigant is the first party, then use the name of the party on the other side of the "v." as your short form. Otherwise thousands of cases would be referred to as <u>State</u> or <u>United States</u> and there would be no way to tell them apart. So, for example, if the case is <u>State v. Hutchcraft</u>, refer to it as <u>Hutchcraft</u>.

You can even shorten the name of the party you use for your short form if you can do so without creating confusion. For example, your short form for the case name <u>Pine River State Bank v. Mettle</u> could be <u>Pine River</u>.

Pinpoint citations: citing or quoting a specific page
Rule 3.2 and 18.3; Bluepages B4.1.2

Whenever you refer to something specific in a case or quote a case, you must cite a specific page. This is called a pinpoint citation or "pincite." If you want to add a pinpoint citation to the full citation the first time you cite a case, put a comma after the page number on which the case begins, followed by the number of the specific page you're citing:

Example 30
```
The court of appeals noted recently that
"the absence of limiting language" in an
employee handbook will prevent an employer
from avoiding liability. Kulkay v. Allied
Stores, 398 N.W.2d 573, 578 (Minn. Ct. App.
1986).
```

Even if the specific page you're referring to or quoting is the first page of a case, you must insert the page number into the full citation:

Example 31
```
"A court of equity will not enter a decree
until all necessary parties are before the
```

```
court." Dougherty v. Keane, 50 F.2d 1013,
1013 (D.C. Cir. 1931).
```

In Example 31, "1013" appears twice: once to show it's the first page of the case and once to show it's the page the quotation comes from.

When you quote from a case that requires parallel citations to two or more reporters, give the specific page for each reporter:

Example 32

```
"An essential element of laches, however,
is that the party asserting it be
prejudiced by the delay." Desnick v. Mast,
311 Minn. 356, 365, 249 N.W.2d 878, 883-84
(1976).
```

The quotation in Example 32 spanned two pages in the *North Western Reporter 2d:* pages 883 and 884. When you cite more than one page, connect the first and last pages cited with a hyphen. Drop digits that are the same in the last page number as the first, but always give at least the final two digits of the last page number.

Note that the period after "delay" in Example 32 goes inside the quotation marks. Periods and commas always go inside the quotation marks. They're small so they fit. Semi-colons and colons, like skis that must go on the roof of your car, always go outside the quotation marks.

Short form citations
Rules 10.9 and 18.8(b); Bluepages B4.2

Once you've cited a case in full, later pinpoint citations can be in short form. In a short-form citation, you omit the parenthetical containing the name of the court and the year. You also omit the number of the page the case starts on. Instead, put in the number of the specific page you're citing. Put "at" before the page number; "p." and "pp." *aren't* used in citations to authority. You can also use a short form of the case name or omit the case name altogether.

Here are three acceptable short-form citations to page 866 of Clemens v. Wilcox, 392 N.W.2d 863 (Minn. 1986):

Example 33
Clemens v. Wilcox, 392 N.W.2d at 866.

Example 34
Clemens, 392 N.W.2d at 866.

Example 35
392 N.W.2d at 866.

The pattern "Clemens at 866" is *not* included as an acceptable short form in rule 10.9.

Use common sense in choosing among these various short forms. If you've mentioned the name of the case recently, then the short form in Example 35 will work:

Example 36
In Clemens, the court held that "personal injury" and "bodily injury" are synonymous. 392 N.W.2d at 866.

Repeating "Clemens" in the citation in Example 36 would be redundant when it already appeared in the preceding sentence. If the case name does not appear nearby, or if there is a risk of confusing the reader, then the short form in Example 33 or 34 would be more appropriate.

If you must use parallel citations in the full citation of a case, you should also use them in any short-form citation. For example, if the full citation is "Smith v. Hubbard, 253 Minn. 215, 91 N.W.2d 756 (1958)," a short form comparable to Example 34 giving parallel citations would be:

Example 37
Smith, 253 Minn. at 225, 91 N.W.2d at 764.

A short form comparable to Example 35 giving parallel citations would be:

Example 38
253 Minn. at 225, 91 N.W.2d at 764.

When you cite a specific page of a case on LEXIS or Westlaw, you use an asterisk followed by the page or screen number: *7. If an electronic database uses paragraph numbers, then use the paragraph symbol followed by the number: ¶ 7. Notice that there's no space between an asterisk and a page number but that there *is* a space between a paragraph symbol and a number.

A short-form citation to a case on LEXIS or Westlaw—according to rule 18.8(b)—has to include some part of the full citation that identifies the database. So a short form of the citation given earlier in Example 11 on page 13 could be:

Example 39
<u>Coteau Servs.</u>, 1988 WL 10171, at *7.

<u>Id.</u>
Rules 4.1 and 10.9(b); Bluepages B4.2

"<u>Id.</u>" (not "<u>ibid.</u>") allows you to shorten your citations even further when you are citing the authority you just cited. Capitalize "<u>Id.</u>" when it starts a citation sentence and—this is the kind of detail *Bluebook* fanatics lie in bed at night wondering about—run the underline under the period.

If you have a general citation followed by a second citation to a specific page, then you must add the page number after the "<u>Id.</u>":

Example 40
An employee handbook can constitute a contract. <u>Pine River State Bank v. Mettle</u>, 333 N.W.2d 622 (Minn. 1983). In <u>Pine River</u>, an employee claimed his discharge was in breach of an employee handbook. <u>Id.</u> at 624.

If the specific page you're citing is the same as the one in the preceding citation, then all you need is "<u>Id.</u>":

Example 41

In <u>Pine River</u>, an employee was discharged
by a bank. 333 N.W.2d at 625. He claimed
his discharge was in breach of an employee
handbook. <u>Id.</u>

Example 42

In <u>Pine River</u>, an employee was discharged
by a bank. <u>Id.</u> at 625. He claimed his
discharge was in breach of an employee
handbook. <u>Id.</u>

You can't use "<u>Id.</u>" if there's another cited authority between
the "<u>Id.</u>" and the authority the "<u>Id.</u>" refers to. *Don't* do this:

Example 43

An employee handbook can constitute a
contract. <u>Pine River State Bank v. Mettle</u>,
333 N.W.2d 622 (Minn. 1983); <u>Kulkay v.
Allied Stores</u>, 398 N.W.2d 573 (Minn. Ct.
App. 1986). In <u>Pine River</u>, an employee was
discharged by a bank. <u>Id.</u> at 625.

Example 43 is wrong because <u>Kulkay</u> comes between the "<u>Id.</u>"
and <u>Pine River</u>, the authority the "<u>Id.</u>" refers to.

You can't even use "<u>Id.</u>" if there's another authority cited *with*
the authority the "<u>Id.</u>" refers to. The following example is also
wrong:

Example 44

An employee handbook can constitute a
contract. <u>Pine River State Bank v. Mettle</u>,
333 N.W.2d 622 (Minn. 1983); <u>Kulkay v.
Allied Stores</u>, 398 N.W.2d 573 (Minn. Ct.
App. 1986). In <u>Kulkay</u>, an employee was
discharged by a department store. <u>Id.</u> at
575.

Even though the "Id." in Example 44 refers to the immediately preceding authority, it's wrong because that authority does not stand alone in the preceding citation.

You can use "Id." in a short-form citation involving parallel citations to specific pages of a case. But the "Id." only takes the place of the name of the case and the volume and name of the reporter in the first of the parallel citations. You still have to give the second of the parallel citations in full. For example, if the full citation is "Smith v. Hubbard, 253 Minn. 215, 91 N.W.2d 756 (1958)," then a short-form citation to specific pages using "Id." would look like this:

Example 45
Id. at 225, 91 N.W.2d at 764.

A short-form citation to a case on LEXIS or Westlaw using "Id." would look like this:

Example 46
Id. at *7.

"Id." can be used for any kind of authority—not just cases. Rule 4.1 gives additional rules and examples.

Rule 4.2 says not to use "supra" to refer to cases, statutes, or constitutions, except in extraordinary circumstances. Since "supra" forces the reader to fish around for an authority you've cited earlier, this rule makes good sense. Use "Id." instead if you can; otherwise use another short form.

Block quotations
Rule 5.1; Bluepages B12.2

Quotations of fifty or more words should be block quotations: indented left and right and single-spaced without quotation marks. Don't attach the citation to the block quotation. Put it on the next double-spaced line following the quotation and then continue with your next text from there.

Except for block quotations, the text of a memorandum or brief will be double spaced. To save space, all the example in this guide are single spaced. But the example that follows appears exactly as it would on your page, so you can see the relation between the double-spaced text and the single-spaced quotation:

Example 47

```
The court in Pine River stated as follows:

    By preparing and distributing its
    handbook, the employer chooses, in
    essence, either to implement or
    modify its existing contracts with
    all employees covered by the
    handbook. Further, we do not think
    that applying the unilateral contract
    doctrine to personnel handbooks
    unduly circumscribes the employer's
    discretion. Unilateral contract
    modification may be a repetitive
    process.

333 N.W.2d at 627. Thus, each new handbook

the employer distributes constitutes a

unilateral modification of the contract.
```

Remember: Don't use quotation marks when you indent a long quotation.

If the first word of the block quotation was indented in the original because it was the first word of a paragraph, then indent it within your indented quotation. Also indent any additional paragraphs if your quotation contains more than one paragraph.

Rule 5.1(b) says that quotations of fewer than fifty words should not be indented and set apart from the rest of the text. But lawyers who want a judge to notice what they're quoting ignore this rule. No matter how short the quotation, if it's the quotation that wins the case, you'll find it indented and single-spaced in a good lawyer's brief (probably with critical words underlined as well).

Changes in quotations
Rules 5.2 and 5.3

When you use a quotation as a phrase or clause in one of your sentences, *don't* indicate that you've omitted language or citations from the beginning or end of the quotation:

Example 48
When the employment is at-will, "the employer can summarily dismiss the employee for any reason or no reason." <u>Pine River</u>, 333 N.W.2d at 627.

The full sentence from which I took this quotation read as follows: "This means that the employer can summarily dismiss the employee for any reason or no reason, and that the employee, on the other hand, is under no obligation to remain on the job."

But if you omit language from within a quotation, indicate it with three periods, called an ellipsis. Separate the periods with spaces, and leave a space before the first period and after the last period:

Example 49
"Where the hiring is for an indefinite term . . . the employment is said to be at-will." <u>Pine River</u>, 333 N.W.2d at 627.

If you omit citations or footnotes from within a quotation, you don't need an ellipsis. Instead, put the phrase "citations omitted" or "footnotes omitted" in a parenthetical at the end of your citation.

When you use a quotation as a full sentence, *do* indicate an omission from the beginning or end. To indicate an omission from the beginning, change the first letter of the first word of your quotation from lower to upper case and put it in brackets.

Never begin a quotation with an ellipsis. To indicate an omission from the end, use four periods. Three of the periods function as the ellipsis and one functions as the period ending the sentence. Language has been omitted from both ends of the following example:

Example 50

```
"[T]he employer can summarily dismiss
the employee for any reason or for no
reason . . . ." Pine River, 333 N.W.2d
at 627.
```

Also use four periods when you omit language from the beginning or end of a sentence within a quotation:

Example 51

```
"Where the hiring is for an indefinite
term, as in this case, the employment is
said to be at-will. . . . [T]he employee is
under no obligation to remain on the job."
Pine River, 333 N.W.2d at 627.
```

To get the spacing right when you use four periods, you must keep in mind which period is the sentence-ending period. If nothing is omitted from the end of a sentence, the sentence-ending period immediately follows the last word. That's why there's no space between "at-will" and the period after it in Example 51. If language is omitted from the end of a sentence, the ellipsis follows the last word. That's why there's a space between "reason" and the period after it in Example 50; there's always a space before the first period of the ellipsis. The sentence-ending period in Example 50 is the one with no space between it and the closing quotation marks.

Also use four periods to indicate that you've omitted one or more entire paragraphs from a long quotation. Indent the four periods and put them on a separate line. Rule 5.3 has additional rules on how to indicate omissions in quotations.

If you underline something in your quotation that was not underlined or italicized in the original, put a phrase such as "emphasis added" in a parenthetical at the end of your citation:

Example 52

When the employment is at-will, "the
employer can summarily dismiss the employee
for any reason <u>or no reason</u>." <u>Pine River</u>,
333 N.W.2d at 627 (emphasis added).

If you add something within a quotation, put it in brackets:

Example 53

"This means that the employer can summarily
dismiss the employee for any reason or no
reason, and that the [at-will] employee, on
the other hand, is under no obligation to
remain on the job." <u>Pine River</u>, 333 N.W.2d
at 627.

5 How to Cite a Statute

Federal Statutes
Rule 12; Bluepages B5.1.1

A basic citation to a federal statute contains the following four elements in this order:

1. the title number;
2. the abbreviated name of the code;
3. the section number;
4. the year on the spine of the code volume (*not* the year the statute was enacted or became effective).

A code is a multi-volume set of books containing all the statutes in a particular jurisdiction grouped by subject matter. Just as cases are published in official and unofficial reporters, statutes are published in official and unofficial codes. Always cite a statute to the official code if possible.

The current official code for federal statutes is the *United States Code,* abbreviated "U.S.C." A basic citation to a federal statute looks like this:

Example 54
30 U.S.C. § 523 (1994).

A citation to an unofficial federal code would contain the same four elements in the same order. Table T1 on page 218 contains the forms for citing an unofficial federal code.

Note that nothing is underlined in a citation to a statute and that the section symbol (§) is used. Put a space between the section symbol and the number that follows it. If you are citing to

33

more than one section, don't use "et seq." Instead, specify exactly which sections you're citing and use two section symbols:

Example 55
```
30 U.S.C. §§ 523-528 (1994).
```

Note that the "5" in "528" isn't omitted as it would be if the hyphen connected two page numbers. Because statutory numbering systems are so varied, rule 3.4(b) says you don't have to shorten the second of two section numbers connected with a hyphen if it will help avoid confusion.

State Statutes
Rule 12; Bluepages B5.1.2

State statutes are often published in an official code and in one or more unofficial codes. If possible, cite state statutes currently in force to the official code. To figure out which state code to cite, turn to the section on the state in table T1 and look under the subheading "Statutory compilations."

For example, if you wanted to know which code to cite for Indiana, you'd turn to the section on Indiana on page 240. Under "Statutory compilations" three codes are listed: the *Indiana Code*, *West's Annotated Indiana Code*, and *Burns Indiana Statutes Annotated*. The state code the *Bluebook* prefers that you cite will always appear first in the list of state codes for any particular state. This is reinforced by the instruction after "Statutory compilations": "Cite to IND. CODE if therein." If your statute did not appear in the *Indiana Code*, you would cite it to the first code on the list in which it did appear.

A basic citation to most state codes contains the following elements in this order:
1. the abbreviated name of the code;
2. the section number of the particular statute (and sometimes the number of the volume it appears in);

3. the year on the spine of the code volume (*not* the year the statute was enacted or became effective).

These elements are laid out for you in the correct form in the right-hand column in table T1 opposite the full names of the codes. All you have to do is fill in the formula given and convert the small caps to ordinary typeface. So a citation to a statute in the Indiana Code would look like this:

Example 56
```
Ind. Code § 483 (1996).
```

When you cite an unofficial state code, you have to include the name of the publisher in the parentheses with the year. A citation to *West's Annotated Indiana Code* would therefore look like this:

Example 57
```
Ind. Code Ann. § 27-1-3-2 (West 1994).
```

Some state codes use subject-matter names in the titles of particular code volumes. For example, turn to the "Statutory compilations" for Maryland on pages 245 and 246. The *Annotated Code of Maryland* has about thirty different subject-matter categories. A citation to that state code following the form given on the right (opposite the name of the code) would look like this:

Example 58
```
Md. Code Ann., Fam. Law § 5-521 (1992).
```

Because the citation form for state codes varies so much, it's a good idea to play it safe and look up the form in table T1.

Other Rules for Citing Statutes

Supplements and pocket parts
Rule 3.1(c)

If your statute appears in a supplement to a bound volume—either a bound supplement or a pocket part—identify the supplement and its year of publication in the parentheses:

Example 59
Minn. Stat. § 181.932 (Supp. 1997).

If part of your statute appears in a bound volume and part of it appears in a supplement to that bound volume, identify both in the parentheses and give the years of publication of both:

Example 60
Minn. State § 176.301 (1996 & Supp. 1997).

Note that in the parentheses the symbol "&" is used instead of the word "and."

Session laws
Rule 12.4

After a legislative session, all the statutes enacted by a legislature during that session are collected in a volume (or volumes) and published. These are the "session laws," and they are arranged chronologically in the order they were passed, rather than by subject. When the session laws are later compiled into a code, they will be rearranged; each statute will be inserted according to its subject in the appropriate part of the code.

You will cite session laws in the following situations: when the statute does not yet appear in a code, when you are referring to the historical fact of a statute's enactment, when the language in the code differs materially from the language in the session laws, and when the statute appears in so many scattered sections of the code that it's impossible to cite the code.

Statutes at Large contains the official federal session laws. A citation to it contains the following information in this order:

1. the name of the statute;
2. the public law number;
3. the volume number, the abbreviation "Stat.," and the page number;
4. the year in which the statute was passed.

Thus:

Example 61
```
National Museum of the American Indian Act,
Pub. L. No. 101-185, 103 Stat. 1336 (1989).
```

Rule 12.4 gives other rules for citing session laws. When constructing a citation to a state's session laws, consult the section on the state in table T1.

Citing a statute to LEXIS or Westlaw
Rule 12.5 and 18.3.2

If you can't cite a statute to a code or its supplements, or to session laws, the next best source is a widely used electronic database like LEXIS or Westlaw. Your citation to a database will look the same as a citation to a code with one exception: Instead of putting the year of the code in the parentheses, you'll put the name of the database and the information the database gives you onscreen about its currency:

Example 62
```
Ind. Code § 483 (LEXIS through 1996
legislation).
```

If the code in the database is not the official code, the name of the publisher goes in the parentheses just as it does with a printed code:

Example 63

```
Ind. Code Ann. § 27-1-3-2 (West, WESTLAW
through 1996 Act 12).
```

Names of statutes and original section numbers
Rule 12.3.1(a)

If a statute is commonly referred to by its name or original section number, or if that information would help the reader identify the statute, you can include it in the citation. Sometimes a statute will have both an official name and a popular name by which it is known. You can use either or both in your citation, in addition to your citation to the official code:

Example 64

```
Employee Retirement Income Security Act of
1974 (ERISA) § 502, 29 U.S.C. § 1132
(1994).
```

Short form for statutory citations
Rule 12.10; Bluepages B5.2

Section B5.2 of the Bluepages allows you some discretion in the use of short forms for citing statutes. While you're still in the general discussion in which the full citation appears, you can use any short form that clearly identifies the statute.

The table in rule 12.10 on page 124 in the *Bluebook* gives examples of acceptable short forms. The alternatives listed under the columns headed "Text" and "Short Citation" are all short forms for the full citations of the statutes. In a memorandum or brief, use the "Text" short forms in your text, and the "Short Citation" forms in your citations.

Now look on page 124 at the first example of a full citation of a named statute: "Administrative Procedure Act § 1, 5 U.S.C.

§ 551 (2006)." The short form you use will depend in part on how this statute is commonly referred to. If it's commonly referred to by its original section number in the Administrative Procedure Act, then it would make sense to refer to that section number in your short forms. In text, those could be "section 1 of the Administrative Procedure Act" or simply "section 1." In a citation, those could be "Administrative Procedure Act § 1" or simply "§ 1." If the statute is commonly referred to by its section number in the *United States Code*, then you would refer to that section number in your short forms.

If you wanted to refer to the entire Administrative Procedure Act in text, after a full citation you could refer to it simply as "the Act":

Example 65
These procedural problems were not anticipated in the Act.

Note that "Act" is capitalized. Rule 8 and Section B7.3 of the Bluepages give other rules on capitalization.

You can also use "Id." for statutory citations. The rules for its use in statutory citations are similar to those for its use in case citations, except that you omit the word "at" when "Id." is followed by a section symbol. For example, if your full citation to a federal statute appeared as "28 U.S.C. § 1332 (2006)," your next citation could appear as:

Example 66
Id. § 1332(a)(1).

Uniform acts
Rule 12.8.4

If you're citing a uniform act itself, use the same form you use for other statutes: first the abbreviated name of the code, then the section number, and finally the year of publication in parentheses. A citation to the Uniform Commercial Code would look like this:

Example 67
U.C.C. § 2-209 (1978).

If you want to cite a section of the Uniform Commercial Code, but as the law of a particular state, then cite the state code just as if you were citing any other state statute:

Example 68
Minn. Stat. § 336.2-209 (1996).

6 How to Cite Other Commonly Cited Sources

Constitutions
Rules 11 and 8; Bluepages B6

A citation to a constitution begins with the abbreviated name of the country or state, followed by the word "constitution" abbreviated "Const.," followed by the abbreviated name and number of the particular subdivision you're citing. Use table T16 to abbreviate the names of subdivisions of constitutions and most other authorities. In table T16 "amendment" is abbreviated "amend.":

Example 69
```
U.S. Const. amend. IV.
```

"Article" is abbreviated "art." in table T16:

Example 70
```
Ariz. Const. art. 2, § 6.
```

Note that "Const." is not in large and small capital letters, and nothing in the citation is underlined.

Rule 11 forbids the use of short forms other than "<u>Id.</u>" for citing constitutions. But you can use short forms when you refer to a constitutional provision in text. When you refer to a subdivision of the U.S. Constitution in text, capitalize the short form:

Example 71
```
The Fourth Amendment no longer effectively
deters police misconduct.
```

Also capitalize "Constitution" in text when you're referring to the U.S. Constitution. Rule 8 gives other rules on capitalization.

Rules of Evidence and Procedure
Rule 12.9.3

These are easy. They require no date, no publisher, no page number—just the abbreviated name of the rule and the rule number:

Example 72
```
Fed. R. Evid. 804.
```

"Fed. R. Evid." in Example 72 is the abbreviation for "Federal Rule of Evidence." The *Bluebook* doesn't require any particular form for abbreviating the names of rules of procedure or evidence. Rule 12.9.3 suggests abbreviations, including "Fed. R. Civ. P." for the Federal Rules of Civil Procedure and "Fed. R. Crim. P." for the Federal Rules of Criminal Procedure. But it says you also may use abbreviations suggested by the rules themselves.

Restatements
Rule 12.9.5

A restatement is cited by giving first its name, then the section number, and finally the year it was adopted or last amended. When you cite a second restatement, write the entire word "Second" (not the abbreviation "2d") in parentheses after the word "Restatement":

Example 73
```
Restatement (Second) of Torts § 90 (1965).
```

If you're citing a comment or illustration in a restatement, indicate that after the section number. According to table T16, the abbreviation for "comment" is "cmt." and the abbreviation for "illustration" is "illus.":

Example 74
```
Restatement (Second) of Torts § 90 cmt. b,
illus. 2 (1965).
```

Administrative Rules and Regulations
Rule 14; Bluepages B5.14

Cite federal rules and regulations to the *Code of Federal Regulations* (C.F.R.) if possible. A citation to C.F.R. contains the following elements in this order:

1. the volume number;
2. the abbreviation "C.F.R.";
3. the section number of the rule or regulation;
4. the year of the code edition you're citing (in parentheses).

Thus:

Example 75
```
20 C.F.R. § 636.7 (1994).
```

Add the name of the rule or regulation at the beginning of the citation if it's commonly known by that name:

Example 76
```
Panama Canal Regulations, 35 C.F.R. § 251.1
(1990).
```

If the rule or regulation does not yet appear in C.F.R., cite the *Federal Register.* If it's not there, cite a looseleaf service. If it's not in a looseleaf service, cite an electronic database.

Rule 14.1 contains several examples of citations to federal administrative materials. To cite state rules and regulations, use these examples as a guide, along with the forms given under the heading "Administrative compilation" for each state in table T1.

Books

Rule 15; Bluepages B8

The category "books," for citation purposes, includes everything from pamphlets to multi-volume treatises, as well as what we all commonly think of as a simple book. "Books" does not include C.J.S., Am. Jur., or A.L.R.

A citation to a book contains the following elements in this order:

1. the volume number, if there's more than one;
2. the author's full name as it appears on the book;
3. the title of the book (underlined);
4. a section or paragraph number if the book is divided that way and a page number if it's not (or if the page number is necessary to prevent confusion);
5. the edition number, if there's more than one (in parentheses);
6. the year of publication (in parentheses with the edition number).

Here's an example containing all six of the above elements:

Example 77

2 Charles E. Torcia, <u>Wharton's Criminal Law</u> § 106 (14th ed. 1979).

Remember that the title of a book is one of the few things you underline. Also, note there's a comma after the author's name; that's the only place a comma is used in the citation.

Supplements and pocket parts are cited for books in the same way as they are for statutes:

Example 78

Frank S. Bloch, <u>Federal Disability Law and Practice</u> § 3.21 (1984 & Supp. 1986).

Consult rule 15 when the book you want to cite has more than one author or otherwise doesn't fit the basic pattern in Example 77 or 78.

Law Review Articles
Rules 16 and 6.1(a); Bluepages B9.1.1 and B9.1.3

A citation to a law review article generally includes the following elements in this order:

1. the author's full name;
2. the title of the article (underlined);
3. the volume number of the law review;
4. the abbreviated name of the law review;
5. the first page number of the article;
6. the year of publication of the law review (in parentheses).

Here's an example containing all the above elements:

Example 79
Brian Leiter, <u>Explaining Theoretical Disagreement</u>, 76 U. Chi. L. Rev. 1215 (2009).

Note the punctuation: There's a comma after the author's name and after the name of the article, but no comma between the page number and the parentheses containing the year. Remember that the title of a law review article is one of the few things you underline.

Also note the spacing used in the abbreviated name of the law review in Example 79. The *Bluebook* contains a detailed rule on spacing, rule 6.1(a). You will most often apply that rule when you cite law review articles. The basic rule is that you don't put spaces between adjacent single capitals:

Example 80

How. L.J.

But you leave a space between a single capital or a group of single capitals and longer abbreviations. That's why in Example 80 there is no space between the "L." and "J." but there is a space between "How." and the "L." Ordinals (such as "2d") are treated as single capitals.

Rule 6.1(a) contains a picky exception to the rule that you don't put spaces between adjacent single capitals. When two or more single capitals refer to a "geographical or institutional entity," they should be set apart from other single capitals:

Example 81

S.C. L. Rev.

This abbreviation stands for the *South Carolina Law Review.* Because South Carolina is a "geographical entity," the "S.C." is set apart from the "L."

You can eliminate any uncertainty about the spacing by looking up the abbreviation for the title of a law review in table T13. Table T13 also contains abbreviations of the names of other commonly cited periodicals. If you want to cite a periodical not listed there, construct its abbreviation using tables T13, T10, and T6 as guides.

Generally when a law review issue is intended to be incorporated into a volume, its numbering starts where the previous issue left off. That way, when several issues are combined into a volume, the pages are numbered consecutively from beginning to end. If a volume of a law review has no volume number, but the pages are still numbered consecutively throughout the volume, use the year of publication as the volume number. When you do this, you'll omit the year in parentheses at the end of the citation because it would be redundant:

Example 82

Frank E.A. Sander, <u>Financial Aid</u>, 1970 U. Tol. L. Rev. 919.

Rule 16.5 explains the changes to make if you cite a periodical in which each issue's pages are separately numbered.

A.L.R.
Rule 16.7.6

The *American Law Reports* (A.L.R.) is treated in citations as a compilation of articles rather than a book. A citation to A.L.R contains the following elements in this order:

1. the author's full name;
2. the word "Annotation";
3. the title of the annotation (underlined);
4. the volume number;
5. the abbreviated title A.L.R. (and series number if any);
6. the page number on which the annotation begins (not the page number on which the annotated case begins);
7. the year the volume was published (not the year in which the annotated case was decided).

Thus:

Example 83

Gregory G. Sarno, Annotation, <u>Advertising as Ground for Disciplining Attorney</u>, 30 A.L.R.4th 742 (1984).

The Record
Rule 10.8.3; Bluepages B7

In a memorandum or brief to a court—especially in the "Statement of Facts" section—you will need to cite the record for every claim you make about the facts of your case. The record may contain deposition or trial transcripts. It may contain documentary exhibits, such as affidavits, letters, or contracts. It also may contain documents prepared by the lawyers in the case, such as interrogatories or memoranda to the court. Finally, it may contain documents prepared by the court, such as orders or memoranda. Bluepages Table BT1 suggests abbreviations for these and other documents commonly found in the record of a case.

Put citations to the record in parentheses after whatever they support. If you're citing a specific page, add "at" followed by the page number.

Example 84

```
Nolan knew the purchase price was stated
incorrectly in the agreement. (Nolan Dep.
at 40.)
```

In Example 84, "Dep." stands for "Deposition." Note that a period comes at the end of the citation and that it is placed inside the parentheses when the citation stands alone as a citation sentence.

If you put the citation within one of your textual sentences, keep it in parentheses:

Example 85

```
Nolan knew the purchase price was stated
incorrectly in the agreement (Nolan Dep.
at 40), but he did not tell this to Stoltz
(Stoltz Dep. at 105).
```

The period after the citation to the Stoltz Deposition in Example 85 is placed outside the parentheses because the citation is within the textual sentence.

If you give two or more citations to support a single fact, put them in a single set of parentheses and separate them with semicolons:

Example 86

```
Nolan knew the purchase price was stated
incorrectly in the agreement. (Nolan Dep.
at 40; Massey Aff. para. 9; Sutton Answer
to Pl.'s Interrog. no. 12.)
```

Section B7 of the Bluepages contains additional examples of citations to the record.